T0130247

Becoming God's Worker Bee

Gem Lieser

Copyright © 2021 Gem Lieser.

All rights reserved. No part of this book may be used or reproduced by any means, graphic, electronic, or mechanical, including photocopying, recording, taping or by any information storage retrieval system without the written permission of the author except in the case of brief quotations embodied in critical articles and reviews.

This book is a work of non-fiction. Unless otherwise noted, the author and the publisher make no explicit guarantees as to the accuracy of the information contained in this book and in some cases, names of people and places have been altered to protect their privacy.

WestBow Press books may be ordered through booksellers or by contacting:

WestBow Press
A Division of Thomas Nelson & Zondervan
1663 Liberty Drive
Bloomington, IN 47403
www.westbowpress.com
844-714-3454

Because of the dynamic nature of the Internet, any web addresses or links contained in this book may have changed since publication and may no longer be valid. The views expressed in this work are solely those of the author and do not necessarily reflect the views of the publisher, and the publisher hereby disclaims any responsibility for them.

Any people depicted in stock imagery provided by Getty Images are models, and such images are being used for illustrative purposes only.
Certain stock imagery © Getty Images.

Scripture taken from the King James Version of the Bible.

ISBN: 978-1-6642-1883-3 (sc)
ISBN: 978-1-6642-1884-0 (e)

Library of Congress Control Number: 2021900393

Print information available on the last page.

WestBow Press rev. date: 01/11/2021

WestBow
PRESS®
A DIVISION OF THOMAS NELSON
& ZONDERVAN

Have you ever heard someone say the words, "well aren't you just as busy as a bee"?

That's because bees are indeed very busy little workers.

A worker bee's whole life purpose is to build the hive, keep it clean and provide food for the hive community.

All workers answer to the Queen bee.
She is the captain of the hive and mother
to all the bees within the hive.

Every morning the workers go out into the world to search for food.

A bee's food is nectar.

Flowers have the nectar bees need.
A bee also collects pollen from the flower and
the pollinated flowers can then grow fruit!

Once back to the hive, the bees only rest at night and then come early morning is back up and ready to search for the harvest once again.

So how can you and I be like the strong worker bees? And who is the captain of all the people we see?

It is God. God is the Father of all the people of the world. Just like the Queen bee is mother to the hive, God is the Father of all the things in the world.

Every person and creature answers to God and
all were created by Him, including the bees!

Much like the worker bees, you have a purpose and job to do for God. Each morning when you wake is the perfect time to say a prayer to thank God for a new day and ask Him what job you are to do that day as you go out into the world.

The bees don't do their job alone and neither will you.

God sent His son Jesus to help each one of us every day!

Jesus is our close friend and it is our job to share His story and God's big love for us with others.

Jesus came to Earth to tell us about God's love and how we can keep safe in that love through believing and keeping His Name in our hearts.

God loved us so much that He sent His only son Jesus to save us, guide us and love us!

As God's worker it is your job to be kind to all the people you know, help others when you see them feeling sad or mad.

It is a good time to share how much God loves them and to let them know they are not alone. They too are part of the kingdom of God, just like the bee is part of its hive.

Just like our friend the bee gathers pollen from the flower to turn into sweet honey, we can gather our family and friends to let them know how God's love will make their hearts sweet like honey!

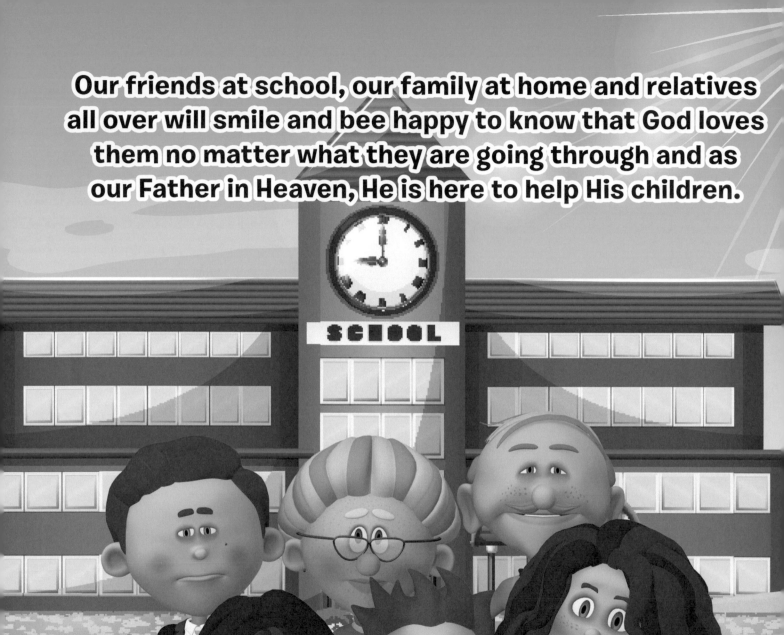

Our friends at school, our family at home and relatives all over will smile and bee happy to know that God loves them no matter what they are going through and as our Father in Heaven, He is here to help His children.

Bees spread pollen to help flowers to give fruit. You can spread kindness, love and Jesus's story to help others hearts blossom like a fruit. Jesus will use that fruit of love to spread to another and another and another!

God gives each of us a job to do for Him.
You can find out exactly how you can
be His helper by asking in prayer.

Prayer is our time to talk to God and
listen to Him speak to our hearts.

This is our job to do each day for God!

God loves you and is ready for you to Bee His!

Ideas and verses to practice with your children or students to go alongside Bee His and enhance young minds knowledge of the Bible and Jesus Christ. Bee His encourages family and classroom discussion on the simple topics of the book with hopes and prayers it stirs in little hearts the joy and purpose in seeking to follow the Lord. Missions, outreach, prayer and praise are all combatants against the cruel and evil of the things in the world. Things that can make young minds weary, broken and confused at an early age.

First and foremost a simple, but powerful verse to share. A New Testament foundation.

John 3:16~~For God so loved the world that He gave His only begotten Son, that whoever believes in him should not perish but have everlasting life.

Ephesians 4:32~~Be kind and compassionate to one another. Discuss ways in which children can show kindness in simple ways, a smile, a hug, opening a door for someone, collecting cans and boxes of food to donate, helping a friend who might be sad or getting picked on by others. And always, the biggest act of kindness is to share Jesus's story with others. John 3:16.

Matthew 9:38~~Ask the Lord of the harvest, therefore, to send out workers into his harvest field. Just like in Bee His as the bees go out daily to collect the harvest and spread the good pollen, the Bible tells us to pray to God to send out workers to collect people that want to learn about Jesus saving us and workers to spread the good news.

Matthew 11:28~~Come to me, all you who are weary and burdened and I will give you rest. Maybe your child has experienced the unfortunate loss of a family member or loved one. Possibly they have a friend who is going through a loss or parent's divorce. This verse can show that God and Jesus want us to bring our sad times, our tears and problems to them so that they can help us heal and rest in the comfort they promise because they love us.

Jeremiah 1:5~~ I knew you before I formed you in your mother's womb. Before you were born I set you apart. This can show a child just how special and individual each one of us are to our creator God. He has plans for us before we were even born. This can help a child feel purpose and fulfillment.

Joshua 1:9~~The Lord your God is with you wherever you go. What better comfort can you offer than the Creator of All Things is with you wherever you go, no matter what! This verse is sweet honey to a lonely heart and also a power building bond between the child and his new adventure seeking the Lord.

Games and group activities are another great way to teach basic Biblical foundations and Jesus' sacrifice for our eternity. Find games that encourage children to learn and hone in on their God given talents and skills. Not only is this confidence building, but can help sharpen their purpose and direction in becoming God's worker bees!

And in ALL things give Praise to God our Father in Heaven! Let those little ones see adults reading the Bible, praying and reaching out in community missions all to God's glory. Amen!

Printed in the United States
By Bookmasters

T0130244

Before you Know it!

Lucy Hawkins

Illustrated by JRaphael Edmundo Honasan

Copyright © 2021 Lucy Hawkins.

All rights reserved. No part of this book may be used or reproduced by any means, graphic, electronic, or mechanical, including photocopying, recording, taping or by any information storage retrieval system without the written permission of the author except in the case of brief quotations embodied in critical articles and reviews.

This book is a work of non-fiction. Unless otherwise noted, the author and the publisher make no explicit guarantees as to the accuracy of the information contained in this book and in some cases, names of people and places have been altered to protect their privacy.

WestBow Press books may be ordered through booksellers or by contacting:

WestBow Press
A Division of Thomas Nelson & Zondervan
1663 Liberty Drive
Bloomington, IN 47403
www.westbowpress.com
844-714-3454

Because of the dynamic nature of the Internet, any web addresses or links contained in this book may have changed since publication and may no longer be valid. The views expressed in this work are solely those of the author and do not necessarily reflect the views of the publisher, and the publisher hereby disclaims any responsibility for them.

Any people depicted in stock imagery provided by Getty Images are models, and such images are being used for illustrative purposes only.
Certain stock imagery © Getty Images.

Interior Image Credit: JRaphael Edmundo Honasan

Scripture taken from the New King James Version®. Copyright © 1982 by Thomas Nelson. Used by permission. All rights reserved.

ISBN: 978-1-6642-1849-9 (sc)
ISBN: 978-1-6642-1850-5 (e)

Library of Congress Control Number: 2021900783

Print information available on the last page.

WestBow Press rev. date: 01/19/2021

WestBow
PRESS®
A DIVISION OF THOMAS NELSON
& ZONDERVAN

To my dearly loved grandchildren: Chloe, Jayla, Summit, Analia, Luna, Sprinter, Yadriel, and Kaiden. You each have a special place in my heart!

Before you know it, the doorbell rings, and here she comes with a great big smile and lots of energy. You have so much to share and a lot to say! There are no endings, just lots of beginnings.

Dancing and singing are in your heart; out comes the microphone and the songs that you love.

With so many books to read and games to play,
the puzzle pieces are scattered all over the place.
But now you are too tired to put anything away.

What now? As the thought of painting comes to mind with no planning or structure, out come the brushes, paper, and paints, with never-ending colors spilling over the paint trays.

With paint on our faces and all over our hands, you have another brilliant thought. "Grandma, can we put up a lemonade stand?"

"Not today, darling; Grandma is too tired. Can you please give me a helping hand?"

It is lunchtime now, and as you eat, there is a lot of time to think about the adventures at the sink.

Dishes turn into boats and spoons into oars;
then the waves in the kitchen sink get rougher,
and puddles spill all over the floor. Oops!

So, I pull out the bucket and mop; then I bring out healthy snacks after cleaning up.

At the table, the child's yawns get bigger, and her eyes begin to close.

There is a moment of quiet snoring that gets louder as I carry the child down the hall.

Well, evening has come, and Mom is at the door. We hug and say goodbye.

And before you know it, a new day will begin. And you will be strolling in again with a great big smile and new ideas for a day of fun.

Behold, children are a heritage from the Lord, the fruit of the womb is a reward.

Psalm 127: 3 (NKJV)

Printed in the United States
By Bookmasters